China

Tradition, Culture, and Daily Life

MAJOR NATIONS IN A GLOBAL WORLD

Books in the Series

Australia
Brazil
China
France
Germany
India
Italy
Japan
Mexico
Russia
South Africa
United Kingdom

China

Tradition, Culture, and Daily Life

MAJOR NATIONS IN A GLOBAL WORLD

John Perritano

Mason Crest

Mason Crest
450 Parkway Drive, Suite D
Broomall, PA 19008
www.masoncrest.com

Printed and bound in the United States of America.

First printing
9 8 7 6 5 4 3 2 1

Series ISBN: 978-1-4222-3339-9
ISBN: 978-1-4222-3342-9
ebook ISBN: 978-1-4222-8582-4

The Library of Congress has cataloged the hardcopy format(s) as follows:

Library of Congress Cataloging-in-Publication Data

Perritano, John.
China / by John Perritano.
pages cm. -- (Major nations in a global world: tradition, culture, and daily life)
Includes index.

ISBN 978-1-4222-3342-9 (hardback) -- ISBN 978-1-4222-3339-9 (series) -- ISBN 978-1-4222-8582-4 (ebook)
1. China--Juvenile literature. 2. China--Social life and customs--Juvenile literature. I. Title.
DS706.P445 2014
951--dc23

2015005024

Developed and produced by MTM Publishing, Inc.

Project Director	Valerie Tomaselli
Copyeditor	Lee Motteler/Geomap Corp.
Editorial Coordinator	Andrea St. Aubin

Indexing Services — Andrea Baron, Shearwater Indexing

Art direction and design by Sherry Williams, Oxygen Design Group

Contents

Introduction 6
1 History, Religion, and Tradition 9
2 Family and Friends 17
3 Food and Drink 25
4 School, Work, and Industry 33
5 Arts and Entertainment 41
6 Cities, Towns, and the Countryside 49
Further Research 56
Series Glossary 57
Index 59
Photo Credits 63
About the Author 64

KEY ICONS TO LOOK FOR:

Words to Understand: These words with their easy-to-understand definitions will increase the reader's understanding of the text, while building vocabulary skills.

Sidebars: This boxed material within the main text allows readers to build knowledge, gain insights, explore possibilities, and broaden their perspectives by weaving together additional information to provide realistic and holistic perspectives.

Research Projects: Readers are pointed toward areas of further inquiry connected to each chapter. Suggestions are provided for projects that encourage deeper research and analysis.

Text-Dependent Questions: These questions send the reader back to the text for more careful attention to the evidence presented there.

Series Glossary of Key Terms: This back-of-the book glossary contains terminology used throughout this series. Words found here increase the reader's ability to read and comprehend higher-level books and articles in this field.

Forbidden City, Beijing, China.

INTRODUCTION

With a population of 1.35 billion people, China is the world's most populous nation, a country brimming in history and overflowing with culture. Despite its rugged geographical isolation marked by brutal deserts, high mountain ranges, and thick rainforests, China has forged over the millennia what is perhaps the world's longest continuous civilization.

In terms of area, China is the third largest country in the world, behind Russia and Canada. Because of its immense size, China is a nation wrapped in many languages, religions, traditions, and cultures.

It is a world that fascinates.

Golden dragons and riverboats.

WORDS TO UNDERSTAND

flourish: to be strong or grow well.

granaries: storerooms for grain.

linchpin: someone or something that is essential for the success of a plan.

monopoly: the control of an industry by one company.

narcotic: a drug that reduces pain and dulls the senses.

CHAPTER 1

History, Religion, and Tradition

The ancient Chinese believed their home was the center of the world, a "Middle Kingdom," which they called Zhongguo. Over time, the Chinese created a massive empire that ushered in a golden age of art, politics, science, and technical innovation. In a span of about 5,000 years, the Chinese succeeded in creating a thriving society that gave the world gunpowder, the magnetic compass, paper, printing, and other discoveries.

Long before those achievements, however, China's first communities were scattered along the country's river valleys, most notably the Huang He, or Yellow River. It is along the Huang He that Neolithic (New Stone Age) farmers found fertile soil and built permanent settlements to exploit the river's natural resources and cultivate crops such as millet, a type of grain.

The first "real" civilization to emerge from the Huang He was the Longshan. The Longshan were the first to build large cities and to organize large-scale public works projects. From about 3000 to 2000 BCE, the Longshan built roads for travel and walls around their cities for protection. In order to complete such enormous tasks, the Longshan developed a complex social system that divided people along class lines.

THE LEGEND OF SILK

Evidence suggests that weaving fabric from the thread of silkworm cocoons was practiced in China around 2600 BCE. And while the exact origins of silk-making technique are shrouded in mystery, it is clear that the skill was first developed in China. Silk weavers would soon perfect this craft and Chinese silk would one day be the envy of the Western world.

By 1766 BCE the first Chinese dynasty, the Shang, emerged in the north. Although the Shang were fierce warriors, they developed a highly sophisticated culture and a complex religion in which they worshipped many gods, including a supreme being they called Shang Di. At first, only the spirits of the king's ancestors could communicate with the Shang gods. Over time, however, others participated in religious rituals.

The Zhou people replaced the Shang and created a vibrant civilization along the Wei River. After conquering Shang armies, the Zhou thrived as a society of writers, teachers, and philosophers, the greatest of whom was named Confucius.

The Zhongshan Iron Bridge over the Yellow River in Lanzhou, China. Today as in ancient times, the river is the center of human activity.

Born around 551 BCE, Confucius came of age while China was in the midst of widespread change. Before Confucius grew to be a philosopher, a person's role in life was predetermined by their lineage. In other words, if your parents were farmers, you would be a farmer, too.

That all changed in the time of Confucius, when people started judging others on their ability, not on their ancestors.

As China grew, the old ways of governing became obsolete as states became larger and ruling over them became more complicated. Rulers started taking advice from people regardless of their station in life, including soldiers, merchants, and farmers.

Confucius—who came from the ruling class—saw what was happening and thought such change was dangerous. He wanted to restore the old order by teaching individuals to be honest, compassionate, and courteous. His influence—Confucianism—still resonates today.

Temples to Confucius, such as this one, can be seen throughout China.

CONFUCIUS IN THE WORLD

Since the 1980s, hundreds of "Confucius Institutes" have formed across the planet, promoting Chinese culture and language instruction. Today, there are more than fifty Confucius Institutes in the United States alone. Confucianism has especially influenced personal, national, and regional life across East Asia, especially in Japan and Korea.

By 221 BCE, much of China as we know it today had become unified under one ruler named Zheng, who proclaimed himself Qin Shi Huangdi, or "First Emperor." A brutal man, Qin Shi Huangdi spent twenty years conquering most of China's warring states and running his empire with an iron fist.

Qin Shi Huangdi undertook massive building projects and allowed education to **flourish**. The modern Chinese bureaucratic state can trace its origins to Qin Shi Huangdi. Qin Shi Huangdi also linked a series of separate walls in the northern part of China and created what we now call the Great Wall. Hundreds of thousands of laborers, mostly slaves, toiled for decades building and repairing the wall. Thousands died. Eventually the wall stretched more than 4,100 miles (6,600 km).

Qin Shi Huangdi's empire collapsed a few years after his death in 221 BCE. Anger over heavy taxes, forced labor, and cruel imperial decisions spilled into

The terra-cotta warriors of China are life-sized clay statues that have been unearthed near the tomb of Qin Shi Huangdi. First found by peasants digging for a well in 1974, archaeologists have since excavated the area and found thousands, with a total likely close to 8,000 figures.

open revolt and the destruction of Huangdi rule. Soon after, the Han dynasty came to power and lasted for more than 400 years.

The policies of the first Han emperor, Gao Zu, a peasant who defeated rival armies, became the bedrock of Han rule, which lasted from around 202 BCE to 220 CE. Under the Han, China soared to new heights. The most famous Han emperor, Wudi (woo dee), trained scholars and built canals, **granaries**, and roads. He reorganized the country's finances, creating a government **monopoly** in the iron and salt trade. His fiscal policies filled the imperial treasury and lessened the tax burden on peasants. Wudi also expanded China's borders, creating outposts in what is today Manchuria, Korea, northern Vietnam, Tibet, and Central Asia.

Wudi also set up a network of trade routes from China to the West, which historians now call the Silk Road. Along the route, grapes, figs, cucumbers, and walnuts, among other goods, traveled from western Asia eastward into China. The Chinese sent silk in the opposite direction. Art, culture, religion, technology, and most every other aspect of civilization traveled along this ancient highway. Eventually the Silk Road spanned 4,000 miles (6,436 km).

The Han invented paper and pioneered the use of ships that could steer using a rudder. They engineered fishing wheels, wheelbarrows, and suspension bridges. Europeans later adapted many of these inventions for their own use, including gunpowder, which they used in weapons.

Gradually China's isolation waned as the West sought to exploit this mysterious country for its riches. By the nineteenth century, British merchants wanted to open China to foreign trade in order to continue the export of opium, a powerful drug used widely in China for its capacity to ease pain and relax the mind. Westerners in Britain and elsewhere had a huge appetite for the **narcotic**. The result was the Opium Wars—the first from 1839 to 1842 and the second from 1856 to 1860—which forced China's rulers to sign treaties opening the country's ports to foreign trade vessels.

Signing the Treaty of Tientsin, 1858, marking an interlude in the Second Opium War.

THE BOXERS

In 1898, a group of Chinese peasants known as the "Righteous and Harmonious Fists," or Boxers, tried to throw the Europeans out of China. They massacred Christian missionaries and killed foreign officials. In response, Great Britain, Russia, France, Italy, Japan, and even the United States sent soldiers to put the Boxer Rebellion down.

It didn't take long for the Western colonial powers, along with Japan, to carve China into "spheres of influence." By the early 1900s, China's imperial system had mostly collapsed in Mongolia, Tibet, and other vassal states, which declared themselves no longer tied to the central government.

The most advanced civilization in world history then degenerated into warring factions along ethnic and cultural lines. Some, such as China's president Sun Yat-sen, believed Chinese culture had to be revived or the nation would die. When he came to power in 1911, Sun Yat-sen abolished China's monarchy and feudal system and established the Republic of China. He guided his country down the road of modernization.

Chiang Kai-shek, who succeeded Sun, became increasingly dictatorial as he sought to modernize China in the mold of liberal Western societies. Although Chiang's government was corrupt, it created independent schools, a free press, independent courts, and trade unions.

Things changed drastically in the 1930s when the Japanese invaded the northern province of Manchuria and later the rest of China on the eve of World War II (1939–1945). When the Japanese retreated in 1945, a civil war between the Nationalists, led by Chiang, and the Communists, who wanted to eliminate the class system, engulfed the country. Communist leader Mao Tse-Tung (Mao Zedong) conquered China in 1949.

Mao tried in vain to transform life through his Great Leap Forward, an attempt to boost the country's agricultural and industrial production. He also instituted the Cultural Revolution, seeking to wipe out China's old customs and ideas while promoting his teachings. Both initiatives failed.

After Mao died in 1976, China's Communist Party opened China up to foreign trade and investment and moved away from a planned economy, the **linchpin** of Communism. As a result, the government shut down many state-run factories and allowed foreign companies access to the Chinese market. By 2010, China had become the world's largest exporter of goods and one of the world's largest economies.

The birthplace of Mao Zedong in Shaoshan, now a tourist destination.

TEXT-DEPENDENT QUESTIONS

1. What were some lasting contributions of the Han dynasty?
2. Why do you think China's first civilizations grew near waterways?
3. Why did foreigners in the nineteenth century seek to exploit China's resources?

RESEARCH PROJECTS

1. Select a Chinese emperor and write a short biography of his life, emphasizing his contributions to the empire.
2. Use the Internet and the library to create a photo timeline of Mao Zedong's life.

Forbidden City, Beijing, China.

A typical Chinese family enjoying playtime together.

WORDS TO UNDERSTAND

concept: a broad, guiding principle.

obedience: the act of obeying.

radically: extremely.

reputation: views that are held about someone.

reverence: respect or adoration.

CHAPTER 2

Family and Friends

The legend is as ancient as its telling. Zi Lu was the most devoted of sons. His family was poor, with little to eat. The boy, a disciple of Confucius, ate wild grass while he traveled hundreds of miles in search of rice for his beloved parents. When Zi Lu's parents died, the boy left his poor village hoping to find work in another part of the country. The king was touched when he heard stories about Zi Lu's *filial piety,* the Confucian ideal that sons and daughters should respect and care for their parents. The king offered Zi Lu a lucrative and comfortable government job. Zi Lu soon grew rich and never had to worry about food or anything else.

Honoring family ties and history is important to China's social fabric. Pictured here is the Ancestral Temple of the Chen Family, or the Chen Clan Academy in Guangzhou, built by the various branches of the Chen family as a place to worship their ancestors and as an educational institution.

Yet, Zi Lu longed for the days when he took care of his parents. "This wealth and honor is flavorless, and depressing," he bemoaned. "How I wish I could return to the old days, when I ate field-greens and carried rice on my back. . . . Now that my parents have left this world I can no longer fulfill my duty as a filial son."

Filial piety, known in Chinese as *xiao*, has always been at the center of Chinese family life. Family is the most important social unit in China, where ancestors are revered and taking care of one's elders is not seen as a burden but a sign of **reverence** and **obedience**. However, in recent years many young people have grown to ignore or at the very least move away from the **concept** of filial piety, which Confucius said was the "root of humanity." As China's economy expands, and as young people move to the cities in search of work, their aging parents complain that they don't see their children as much as they should. The elderly feel lonely and abandoned. For them, filial piety is slowly disappearing.

TRADITIONAL VALUES

Confucius said that every relationship, even between friends, is based on responsibility and obligation. "Never contract friendship with a man that is not better than thyself," he said. "I do not want a friend who smiles when I smile, who weeps when I weep; for my shadow in the pool can do better than that."

As a result, the government in 2013 enacted a law aimed at forcing adult children to visit their aging parents. Known as the "Protection of the Rights and Interest of Elderly People," the law forces children to provide for the "spiritual needs of the elderly." The law states that children should go home "often" to see their parents, while occasionally sending them greetings. Companies are obligated to give employees time off so workers can visit their families. The law, while controversial, seeks to maintain filial piety in a complicated modern world. According to the China's state-run news agency, 185 million people aged sixty and older live far from their children.

If family is the most important and dynamic social unit in China, then the father is its central figure and marriage is its cornerstone. It's the father's job to protect, provide, and educate his loved ones. However, fathers no longer have absolute control over the family as they once did. In fact, in many households, females make all the major financial decisions.

Filial piety—a traditional value that places great faith in honoring parents and grandparents—is still a powerful force in China. Here three generations of a family are enjoying leisure activity in Fuxing Park in Shanghai.

Before modern times, the male was the head of household in China and the most important member of the family, as seen in this 1862 print.

Just as the father's role is changing, customs relating to marriage and romantic relationships are as well. In earlier times, marriage was a matter of survival, arranged by parents based on the wealth and social status of the would-be bride or groom. Wealthy parents never let their children marry a poor person or someone who was not their social equal. These traditional marriages often favored the male's family by allowing the paternal family line to continue.

ARRANGING A MARRIAGE

In an arranged marriage, when the would-be groom's parents decide to make a match, they invite a matchmaker to make the proposal to the girl's family. If the would-be bride's parents agree, the matchmaker, who is usually a woman, is given gifts and a feast is held in her honor to show the families' gratitude.

But indeed, while many Chinese refuse to marry without their parents' consent, arranged marriages are more and more outdated. Moreover, there has been steady growth in the number of men and women marrying foreigners, a situation that was unheard of until thirty or so years ago. During Mao's Cultural Revolution, the government outlawed all foreign, mixed marriages. In 1978, there was not a single registered mixed marriage in China. Yet, by 2012, that number skyrocketed to 53,000 as Chinese society gradually underwent seismic cultural reforms. Mao's government even banned kissing and holding hands in public. People now hold hands in the streets and women are far more aggressive in dating situations.

However, the structure of the Chinese family has grown increasingly complicated because of the country's "one-child" policy. When the Communists took control of the Chinese government in 1949, they urged people to have more babies. Government officials reasoned that more children meant more workers and ultimately a stronger economy. China's population grew so quickly that it outstripped the government's ability to feed, educate, and house its citizens. In response, the government tried several unsuccessful programs to lower the birthrate.

In 1979, China implemented the one-child policy, rewarding couples who birthed only one child and fining those that had more. There were exceptions, however. The government allowed rural families and ethnic minorities to have two children without fining them. Many consider the law unfair. In fact, wealthy couples routinely break the law because they can afford to pay the fine. Efforts to **radically** overhaul the policy, or do away with it completely, have fallen short in recent decades.

ONE CHILD, FOR GOOD OR BAD

The Chinese say the country's one-child policy has prevented 400 million births since 1979, while improving the lives of millions. However, some experts say the policy has been so successful that it is complicating China's economic future. Its population is rapidly aging, a fact that may hamper China's growth as more people look to the government for support.

Traditional marriages and dating practices are fading in China, particularly in major cities. Here a couple holding hands enjoys a day in a Beijing park.

Two young professionals greet in Beijing. Interpersonal obligations and connections are an important aspect of business in China.

Although families play a paramount role in Chinese culture, friendships are also important. Like most everything else in China, Confucianism greatly influences friendships and other relationships. However, friendship in China is different from friendship in Western cultures. In the West, the focus is on the "individual," while in China the focus is on "community."

One of China's most important cultural traits is the term they use for relationship: *guanxi*. The word means "personal contacts" or "personal connections." It also means a special association in which one person can make unlimited demands on the other. Through the concept of *guanxi*, people bond because of their obligations to one another. *Guanxi* is often established by schoolmates, neighbors, and others who share a commonality, such as school, work, or a neighborhood. Nothing in China can be accomplished without *guanxi*. It is a way to network, to connect with others, and it is routinely used in business.

Reqing is a related concept that guides personal relationships. Translated as "human feelings," *reqing* means that if a person does you a favor, then you owe that person a favor in return.

The concept of *lian*, or "face," is also deeply rooted in Chinese culture. *Lian* is a metaphor for a person's **reputation**. Someone who "has face" has a good reputation. People can also give others *lian*. For example, if a popular child plays with another child who is new in the neighborhood, the popular child helps improve the new person's reputation. As a result, the new child's social standing within his or her peer group is elevated. In the business world, companies often choose to do business with larger international firms to enhance their reputation or to "gain face."

TEXT-DEPENDENT QUESTIONS

1. Why would a Chinese businessman not want to "lose face" during a contract negotiation? Explain your answer.
2. Explain how China's 2013 law aimed at forcing adult children to visit their aging parents conforms to the Confucian idea of filial piety.
3. What might have motivated China's Communist government to encourage people to have as many children as they could?

RESEARCH PROJECTS

1. Research the population of China and create a graph or chart that you will then share as a simple handout or display on a computer.
2. Research the rituals of a traditional Chinese marriage. Next, interview a married couple that you might know, such as your parents, grandparents, friends, or other relatives, and compare their courtship rituals to the Chinese. What are the differences? Are there any similarities?

A family enjoys a traditional Chinese meal.

Three generations gather at mealtime.

WORDS TO UNDERSTAND

advocated: supported or promoted.

aromatic: pleasant smelling.

imported: bringing something in from another country.

mesmerized: fascinated.

regional: related to a specific area.

CHAPTER 3

Food and Drink

The famous Venetian explorer, Marco Polo, was one of the first westerners to enjoy the mysterious culinary delights of China. In fact, according to legend, Marco Polo brought back to Italy spaghetti noodles from China. While it's true the Chinese invented the noodle some 4,000 years before Marco Polo's visit, there's no evidence to suggest that he introduced the thin strands of cooked dough to Europe.

Still, upon Marco Polo's return to Venice, Europeans were **mesmerized** to read about the Chinese pasta-like dishes that he enjoyed. Today, 700 years after Marco Polo made his famous journey, the Western world is still fascinated with Chinese cuisine. In 2006, China globally exported $2.5 billion worth of food ingredients—a 150 percent increase from 2004. In 2012, the United States **imported** $426 million worth of food from China.

AN ANCIENT BOWL OF NOODLES!

In 2005, scientists found the oldest bowl of noodles in an ancient Chinese tomb, suggesting that the Chinese, not the Italians, invented the noodle. The noodles were thin and yellow and were found in a long-buried overturned bowl in northwest China. Scientists determined the noodles to be about 4,000 years old. The ancient cooks made the strands from two kinds of millet. Scientists say the size and thinness of the noodles show a high degree of culinary sophistication.

Food is very special to the Chinese and reflects the country's ethnic and **regional** differences. While people in the southern part of the country rely on rice as a staple, those in the north eat food mostly made from grain. The provinces of Sichuan, in the country's center, and Hunan, to Sichuan's east, are famous for hot and spicy food, while the residents of Guangdong, on China's southern coast, eat food that is much milder.

Hot and spicy ramen from the Sichuan region.

Although customs vary from place to place, Chinese families generally eat three meals a day. As westerners eat specific foods at different times, such as eggs and bacon for breakfast, the Chinese eat the same food regardless of the time.

Rice balls served in a bamboo steamer.

Like many other facets of Chinese culture, the nation's relationship to food has undergone a tremendous metamorphosis over the centuries. During the Pre-Qin period (2100–221 BCE), China was a land in turmoil. Many of the era's great thinkers, including Mozi, also known as "Master Mo," thought often about food and life. Mozi **advocated** that people should eat only to survive. "When it comes to food, there should be no more than suffices to replenish one's energy and fill the empty spaces: all that is required to strengthen the body and satisfy the stomach," he said.

Confucius offered a more expanded view. He believed dining was essential to social well-being. He said while "the foremost function of eating was physical and mental cultivation, it should also be undertaken to strengthen kinship and friendship."

STICKY RICE

Rice is a staple of most Chinese meals, but the rice in China is much different from rice in the West. In Asia, the grains of rice are short or medium in length. They become gummy or "sticky" when cooked. In the West, the grains of rice are long and become fluffy when boiled.

It was that Confucian ideal that dominated mealtime then and still today. For example, the order a person sits at the dinner table, whether with family, with friends, or in other situations, is a demonstration of that person's social status within that particular group. The left side of the table is reserved for the most honored members of the group. In addition to social rules governing food and dining, there is a spiritual dimension to eating also. The Chinese have always believed that food has more mystical qualities than simply providing sustenance. An abundance of food indicates good fortune, and good cuisine is considered essential for good health.

Regardless of what one thinks about the social or spiritual implications of food and eating, Chinese food was—and is—varied, **aromatic**, and delicious. The Chinese cookbook contains just about anything that is edible. Virtually nothing is taken off the table. While taste and aroma are important, the presentation of a dish is equally desirable. To make food pleasing to the eye, Chinese cooks use ingredients of different colors, each mixed in the right combinations. Chefs also employ a variety of techniques to cook the food, including stir-frying, roasting, steaming, deep-frying, and simmering. The goal is to preserve the natural taste of the ingredients.

The Confucian ideal of filial piety plays a dominant role at the dinner table. The finest food is served first to the oldest family members as a sign of respect. Parents teach their children to eat equally from each dish even though they might like one type of food better than the other dishes. It is rude to leave the slightest speck of flood on the plate.

Dried fish and other exotic ingredients are sold in the Chinese market in New York City, where many ethnic groups live side by side and continue their traditions.

Most Chinese do not use napkins, opting instead to use a hot towel to clean themselves at the end of the meal. Unlike in the West where slurping soup is rude, the Chinese have no qualms about such eating habits. They slurp to cool the soup and to diffuse its flavor.

The food's presentation is also important. Traditionally there is a strict etiquette as to where each dish is placed on the table and the angle the dish is supposed to be turned. The server must turn his or her head away if they speak so as not to have their mouth open above the food.

Filial piety is important at family meals too.

The Chinese rarely drink beverages during their meals. That's because tea is served throughout the day. Soup is usually the only liquid. Meats and vegetables are served as side dishes, while *hsia fan*, "a period of grain," is the main course. In the south and cities, *fan* might be rice, while in the north it could be cooked whole grains, noodles, or breads.

Banquets are boisterous affairs held to celebrate important events such as the New Year, the Moon Festival, weddings, and other occasions. Special treats, such as moon cakes for the Moon Festival or New Year's pudding, are served. During a celebration all the food is served at the same time. Meats and vegetables are now the main courses—and there are several—while diners eat *fan* at the end of the meal. Before people start digging in, and despite the abundant fare, the host will usually "apologize" for a meager meal.

A moon cake, filled with red bean paste, is eaten during the Moon Festival in mid-autumn.

TEA FOR THE AGES

Tea is the beverage of choice. At first, people ate tea leaves and used them in medicine. It wasn't until the Han dynasty, some 2,000 years ago, that people began drinking tea brewed from the leaves. By the mid-1300s, Europeans discovered the drink, making it popular in the West. Today, Turkey is the world leader in tea consumption, drinking nearly 7 pounds per person each year. Ireland comes in a distant second at 4.83 pounds. The Chinese drink only 1.25 pounds per person, but that's because tea is expensive.

Tea is an important part of Chinese culture.

Whether eating a simple family meal or an elaborate feast, all Chinese use chopsticks, rather than forks and spoons. The Chinese have been using chopsticks since around 1200 BCE. The utensils were so important that the earliest set scientists have discovered was bronze and found in an ancient tomb in Henan Province.

Ancient cooks used chopsticks to reach into boiling pots of water or oil. It wasn't until 400 CE that people began using the utensils to eat. At the time, China was undergoing a population boom, and carving chopsticks from wood was one way for families to save money. Chefs cut meat and vegetables in tiny pieces to save on cooking fuel. The diminutive size of the food made it perfect for chopstick use.

Confucianism also played a role in the evolution of the chopstick. Confucius believed that sharp utensils, such as knives and forks, would remind people of where food came from—the slaughterhouse. He also believed a sharply tipped knife was a reminder of war and violence. Confucius believed such utensils would ruin dinner. As his teachings snaked across Asia, more and more people began using chopsticks. Unlike Japanese chopsticks, which are pointy at the tip, Chinese chopsticks are blunt.

Chopsticks are used throughout China, although forks are now available in some restaurants.

TEXT-DEPENDENT QUESTIONS

1. If you lived in China, where would you seat your grandparents at the dinner table? Explain your answer.
2. Explain how Confucianism affected mealtime in China, not only in the past but in the present.
3. Why is there such a diversity of food in China?

RESEARCH PROJECTS

1. Research the different types of food in each region of China and create a computer-generated slide show that explains the culinary similarities and differences between each area.
2. Create a visual step-by-step guide on the best way to use chopsticks. Share the guide as a simple handout or by using the computer.

Traditional ramen soup.

A light rail station in Wuhan, the capital of the Hubei Province in central China.

WORDS TO UNDERSTAND

burgeoning: growing and expanding quickly.

critiqued: reviewed someone's work.

festivities: celebrations.

literacy: the ability to read and write.

transition: change from one condition to another.

CHAPTER 4

School, Work, and Industry

Attending school and receiving a good education is a full-time job for China's students. Education is a way to ascend the social ladder, a means to a good economic life. Because competition is tough, only the best can go to college. That is why each student's life revolves around schoolwork and studying. This focus on education has helped China to develop one of the most dynamic economies of the world.

China's **literacy** rate matches that of many of the world's developed countries, nearly 95 percent for those aged fifteen and older. The country's gross national product, a measure of all the products and services a country's citizens produce in a year, has quadrupled in the past ten years, which experts

Science is an important part of a Chinese education. Here, a student performs a physics experiment.

say is partly the result of China's increasingly educated workforce.

Education in China is a work in progress. When the Republic of China was founded in 1911, reformers based China's educational system on the Western European model, in which the state controlled all levels of learning. After the Communist takeover in 1949, the government abolished the curriculum to teach Communist doctrine and the writings of Mao, China's ruler.

When Mao died in 1976, China's Communist leaders sought to overhaul the educational system once again. Another change swept through in 1986, when the government made it mandatory that children between the ages of six and fifteen must attend school for nine years. Students spend six years in the primary grades and three years in junior middle school. After junior middle school, students can either attend a traditional senior middle school or enroll in a vocational school.

EDUCATIONAL REFORM?

Critics say that China's educational system needs to be overhauled once again. Many believe students are graduating without the creative skills to compete in the global marketplace. They say that rote memorization, the hallmark of any Chinese classroom, crushes a student's individuality and that reliance on exams is not the best way to measure a student's progress.

Children in primary schools attend class five days a week, nine hours a day. The school year runs for nine and a half months, while summer vacation lasts for only a month beginning in mid-July. Students also get a week or so off in October to celebrate China's national holiday. The Chinese New Year is also a school holiday. Students have one to three weeks off.

While in primary school, students must study Chinese, mathematics, physical education, music, art, nature, morals and society, and practical work classes. Chinese and math are often called "The Big 2," which is why 60 percent of class time is devoted to these subjects.

Middle school, in which students learn history, literature, math, and English, prepares students to go to senior middle school (high school) and college, where the competition is greatest because of a limited number of spots. To this end, every summer students take the *gaokao,* China's national college entrance exam. Unlike students in the United States who take similar tests, Chinese high school students prepare their entire academic lives for the exam, also known as the National Higher Education Entrance Examination. In 2014, 9.39 million students took the three-day test, with about 6.98 million students going on to college. In Japan, students take a similar two-day test, although officials are considering scrapping the exam and replacing it with achievement tests throughout high school.

The test is so important to the Chinese that the government rearranges flight paths for planes and traffic patterns for cars so the vehicles do not disturb students as they take the test. In fact, during the 2008 Summer Olympics in Beijing, China's capital, the Olympic torch relay was rerouted around schools so the **festivities** wouldn't bother students.

Class time in China is much different from class time in the West. Unlike the United States, where teachers focus on the individual student, Chinese teachers focus on the entire class. If a Chinese student has difficulty grasping a math concept, the teacher will order the student to come to the front of the class and solve

Collection of chinese symbols and letters.

The entire class will help as a student solves a difficult problem on the blackboard.

the problem with their classmates' help. American students are rarely called to the front of the class to be **critiqued** by the teacher and fellow students.

In China, teachers encourage competitiveness between students. In their view, every student can be successful in every subject, although some might have to work harder than others.

Learning does not stop at the end of the school day. Chinese parents are involved in their children's education. They make certain their children complete their homework assignments. In fact, if a child is sick and cannot go to school, their mother may sometimes go to class and take notes.

The emphasis on education has helped China **transition** from an agricultural society to one that is more technology and industry driven. The process began when Mao died. Upon his death, the Communist Party began reforming and "opening" China's society, a concept known in Chinese as *gaige kaifang*.

AN EXPORT GIANT

China exported $2.2 trillion worth of products in 2013. The top exports are electronics, machinery, clothing and accessories, furniture, lighting, signs, prefabricated buildings, and medical equipment.

Under *gaige kaifang*, (literally, "reform and opening up") the government began allowing foreign trade and investment as the country moved from a centralized economy. In the Communist system, China's economy hinged on the government's control of all aspects of production and consumption, including collective farms and the allocation of individual workloads. These days, the government regulates much less: it allows market competition and consumption to determine types of products, levels of production, and the like.

These changes seem to have paid off. Over the last forty years or so, China has slowly become more integrated into the world's economy. In the 1990s, China joined the World Trade Organization (WTO), which makes sure trade flows smoothly. In order to gain access to global markets, the WTO required China to open its borders to more foreign imports.

Steel workers at a new construction site in Hangzhou, in eastern China.

Today, fueled by several key industries, including energy, manufacturing, and steel, China is the world's largest exporter of goods and the world's second largest economy. Automobiles are big business in China, and in 2013 the Chinese manufactured 21.98 million vehicles. Many foreign carmakers are happy about the **burgeoning** car market in China. General Motors, an American company, sold 3.16 million vehicles in China in 2013, up 11.4 percent from the previous year, while Japanese carmaker Toyota expected to sell 1.1 million vehicles in 2014, up 20 percent from 2013.

The Pudong Lujiazui business and economic center in Shanghai—a symbol of the economic vitality of the city and China itself.

The Three Gorges Dam, the world's largest hydroelectric dam, was constructed to generate power for China's fast-growing population.

ENERGIZING THE ECONOMY

Renewable energy is the fastest growing sector of China's economy. To that end, China boasts the world's largest hydroelectric dam, the Three Gorges Dam, located in Hubei Province in east-central China. The dam spans the Yangtze River and is 1.4 miles (2.3 km) wide and 610 feet (186 m) tall. It holds back so much water that it created a huge lake nearly 410 miles (660 km) long. To build the Three Gorges Dam, some 1.3 million people had to find new homes. Many villages and forests had to be ripped apart during construction.

In addition to automobiles, Chinese factories also build power-generating equipment such as gas turbines and energy transmission equipment. China's steel industry, which was at one time nonexistent, is now the world's largest. In June 2014, the Chinese were churning out 2.31 million metric tons of steel per day, a 1.7 percent increase over May. In the first six months of 2014, China produced 411.91 million tons of crude steel, 3 percent more than the previous year.

The emergence of China as a global economic powerhouse, however, has created cramped conditions in the cities. In 1980, fewer than 200 million people lived in China's cities. That number skyrocketed to nearly 700 million in 2008, which is more than the combined populations of the United States, the United Kingdom, France, and Italy.

TEXT-DEPENDENT QUESTIONS

1. Do you think that teachers in the United States should foster competition among students as they do in China? Explain your answer.
2. Explain how your school day differs from a school day in China.
3. What are some of the problems caused by China's rapid industrialization?

RESEARCH PROJECTS

Think about how much time you spend during the school week doing various activities. Create a table with days of the week down the first column and types of activities across the top to help you analyze your activities. Consider that in China, each student will spend an average of 58 minutes doing homework; 87 percent will spend 27 minutes reading books not associated with their studies; and 45 percent will spend 13 minutes doing community service. Compare your activities to those of the Chinese. What can you conclude?

Boxes stamped "Product of China" ready to be shipped from a factory.

A troupe performing Shaolin kung fu.

WORDS TO UNDERSTAND

celebratory: festive.

embodiment: representation of something's core values and meaning.

humility: quality of being modest or respectful.

immigrant: a person who comes to a country to take up permanent residence.

modernization: the process of becoming modern.

pastime: an activity or interest that a person pursues at his or her leisure.

CHAPTER 5

Arts and Entertainment

Mickey Mouse and Confucius are as different as, well, Mickey Mouse and Confucius. Yet that didn't stop Disney, the global entertainment company, from building a $5.5 billion resort in Shanghai, the first major theme park on the Chinese mainland. The company's decision to build the resort was a major milestone in a nation that once shunned all things Western—including American cartoon characters. In fact, many U.S. companies, including Sea World, Warner Bros., and Six Flags, plan to build fifty-nine theme parks in China within the next decade or so.

Art and entertainment are big business in China, yet such leisure activities cannot be separated from the country's history, ethnicity, or heritage. In the past, people enjoyed themselves by flying kites, playing chess, hunting, story-

Workers on break from their restaurant jobs enjoy a game of mahjong in Pengzhou, Sichuan.

Basketball, now a popular sport for young people, played in the National Stadium in Pengzhou.

telling, dancing, or riding a bicycle. **Celebratory** festivals complete with food, music, games, and drink served as a form of religious and ethnic entertainment, which allowed communities to bond.

A POPULAR PASTIME

Mahjong is one of the most popular games in China. The game is usually played by four people, with 144 tiles marked with various characters and drawings. The object is to build sets by drawing new tiles and discarding others. Mahjong clubs provide people with an important venue for social interaction. Older residents often sit on benches on crowded street corners playing the game.

As China modernizes, there has been a gradual shift from these time-honored recreational pursuits to more twenty-first-century activities. Although people still fly kites and play chess or mahjong, they can also play video games, go see the latest action movie from the United States, or even ride a roller coaster.

Despite this embrace of the West, traditional art and entertainment, such as the Beijing Opera, continue to be immensely popular. Chinese opera, like the theater of the ancient Greeks, is one of the world's oldest forms of dramatic art.

Established during the Tang dynasty (618–907 CE), Chinese opera evolved from traditional folk songs, dances, and music. Many consider the Beijing Opera, which formed about 200 years ago, as the **embodiment** of Chinese culture. The opera combines song, dance, dialogue, and the martial arts. Each Beijing Opera is also a lesson in Chinese history, with important facts and events highlighted in each production.

At a performance of the Beijing Opera, theatergoers can tell who the characters are by *lianpu,* or the art of face painting. Actors paint their eyes, foreheads, and cheeks like the wings of butterflies, birds, or bats. The colors vary depending on the character. Black represents a person that is honest, while white means cunning. Actors also use masks made from ceramic, paper, and tissue. Costumes are colorful and fashioned from silk and satin. The roles of the actors fall into four categories: *sheng,* the lead male character; *dan*, female roles; *jing*, the painted-face male; and *chou*, the clown, one of the opera's main characters.

The Beijing Opera Troupe performing *Farewell to My Concubine* at the Huguang Theatre in Beijing, November 2010.

A CHINESE *ROMEO AND JULIET*

One of the most popular Chinese operas is the *Butterfly Lovers.* The opera is the tale of two fourth-century Chinese lovers who could not get married because of family differences. Sound familiar? The story is often called "China's Romeo and Juliet."

Another style of opera, the Sichuan, originated at the end of the Ming dynasty (1368–1644). It brought together the customs of **immigrants** who flooded Sichuan at the time. The hallmark of the Sichuan opera is the practice of face changing. First used by the ancient Chinese to drive away wild animals, actors don masks that illustrate different emotions. Some actors can put on ten masks in twenty seconds with the raise of a hand, the wipe of a sleeve, or the tossing of a head.

It's no wonder that in a country as old as China, sports would dominate leisure time activities. In fact, if the experts are correct, the Chinese invented an early form of soccer, *cuju*, during the sixteenth century BCE. Poets waxed philosophical about the game, while writers found symbolism in the playing field (earth) and the ball (a star or planet). The twelve players represented the zodiac. The first *cuju* ball was made from stone to help soldiers become physically fit. Peasants, the wealthy, men, children, and women all played the game. *Cuju* is being revived today, especially as soccer becomes more important to fans of the sport in China and across the world.

This painting depicts children possibly playing *cuju*, an early form of soccer.

Bahe, or tug-of-war, is another popular **pastime**, a traditional game first played during the Lantern Festival, which falls during the first lunar month as part of the festivities to bring in the New Year—usually in Febru-

Dragon boat racing in Victoria Harbor in Hong Kong.

ary or March. Neighboring villages competed against one another. The game is still played in many countries and was an Olympic sport from 1900 to 1920.

For those with a need for speed, dragon boat racing is popular. Many cities around the world with big populations of Chinese immigrants, including New York and Boston, host dragon boat events. The sport, in which teams of rowers race one another in boats decorated as dragons, commemorates the life and death of the ancient poet Qu Yuan, who lived from 340 to 278 BCE.

Before his death, Qu Yuan called for social and political reform in his home state of Chu, but the king refused to listen. Instead, the king exiled Qu. In 278, Qu drowned himself after hearing that troops had invaded Chu. People rushed to the river to save him and threw steamed rice wrapped in leaves into the water as a sacrifice to his spirit.

Kung fu is another ancient sport still popular today. Kung fu, as with other martial arts, originated as a form of protection against wild animals. At its heart, it utilizes kicks, blocks, and open and closed hand strikes as a means of personal defense. There are many styles and substyles, including Shaolin kung fu, which emphasizes kicks and open stances.

Kung fu is not just a set of fighting skills. It resonates philosophically. Its literal translation describes any person that accomplishes a goal through hard work; a way for people to find inner peace. The techniques grew alongside Confucianism and Taoism, a philosophy in which people believe individual power flows through all living and nonliving things. In fact, it is the Taoist concept of "yin and yang," the idea that opposite forces complement one another, that informs many kung fu techniques. Buddhism, imported from India during the years 58–76 CE, also plays a role by underscoring **humility** and restraint.

MARTIAL ARTS AND THE MOVIES

Movies and television shows, including *The Simpsons,* have popularized the type of kung fu practiced by the warrior monks of Shaolin. Shaolin is one of the most famous Buddhist monasteries in the world, built in 477 or thereabouts. It is there that the Indian sage Bodhidharma established the Zen school of Buddhism. The monks' brand of kung fu mixes physicality with Buddhist spiritualism.

Tai chi is another martial art rooted deep in Chinese history. Tai chi, which some people believe dates back 2,500 years, involves slow body movements to promote inner peace and calmness. Some tai chi masters are able to throw an opponent down with lighting speed and with minimal effort. Today, tai chi is tied to good health and meditation. It allows people that are stressed to calm the body and the mind.

The Chinese are also proficient table tennis players, and China's national team has won every world championship except two since 1971. The Chinese also dominated the game in the 2008 and 2012 Olympics.

Despite **modernization** and the effects of globalization, Chinese leisure activities are still marked by traditional activities. Perhaps the most well known and popular is the fifteen-day celebration of the New Year, also known as the Spring Festival. The celebration takes place after the second new moon of the year, or sometime between January 21 and February 19. During that time, families gather in homes to celebrate, while workers in other cities return to their hometowns. Most workplaces shut down. Extensive feasts are the centerpiece of this unique festival, as are fireworks and parades showing off the Chinese zodiac animal that the New Year honors.

A China Table Tennis Super League match in 2013.

TEXT-DEPENDENT QUESTIONS

1. Do you think U.S. entertainment companies will have a negative or positive impact on Chinese culture? Explain your answer.
2. Explain the influence of Taoism and Buddhism on kung fu.
3. Explain the importance of *lianpu*, or the art of face painting, in the Beijing Opera.
4. How do entertainment and the arts help the Chinese stay connected to their past?

RESEARCH PROJECT

Research a modern game or sport that had Chinese origins and then write an essay about that sport.

Practicing tai chi in a park in Liuzhou, in southern China.

The historic town of Fenghuang in Hunan, China.

WORDS TO UNDERSTAND

bastion: center or stronghold.

cornerstone: vital thing or person.

defensive: designed for military protection.

ensemble: group of performers.

indigo: a plant used to dye cloth blue.

industrialization: transition from agriculture to industrial activity.

CHAPTER 6

Cities, Towns, and the Countryside

Fly over China and you will see a coastline that is flat and a good place to build harbors for oceangoing ships. Soar over China's mountains and you will see some of the tallest, most rugged peaks on the planet. Hike along its Great Wall and you will encounter some of the most world's most forbidding **defensive** structures. Travel through China's cities and you will see some of the most modern cities in the world, gleaming mountains of steel and glass, canyons of concrete and light, and crowded boulevards.

China is big, expansive, and diverse. From its deserts to its plateaus, from its mountains to its seacoast, no one word and no one phrase can adequately describe the rugged beauty and sheer immenseness of the country. With a land area of about 3.7 million square miles (9.6 million square km), China is the third largest nation behind Russia and Canada. China is a land brimming with booming cities and exotic villages.

SACRED LANDSCAPES

China is home to many sacred Buddhist mountains. Chief among them is Mount Emei in Sichuan Province. Buddhists regard the mountain as a place of enlightenment. Mount Emei is no ordinary mountain. It is home to China's first Buddhist temple and seventy-six monasteries. Some are built on terraces, while others stand on stilts.

Villages were once the heart of China, the keepers of ancient traditions, the places where most people lived. However, China's fast-paced economic growth has made the cities the center of Chinese society. Beijing, the capital of China, is one such center. Famous as a destination for travelers seeking to understand what makes China tick, it is both an ancient and modern city. Established more than 3,000 years ago, the city became the capital in 1272. Inside Beijing is the Forbidden City. Built 600 years ago, it was once the imperial palace of Ming dynasty rulers.

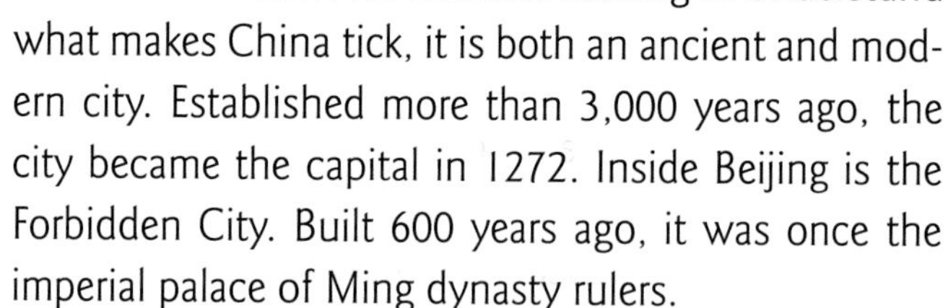

Since its emergence as a global power, China's cities, such as Beijing, Shanghai, Wuhan, and others, have gone on a building binge. In 1978, no Chinese city had more than 10 million people and only two had 5 million. Today, there are six cities with a population of more than 10 million, and ten additional cities have a population of between 5 million and 10 million. In fact, more than 680 million people now live in the cities, which is more than half of China's population.

You can see this growth spurt everywhere, especially in Wuhan, a bustling metropolis of 10.2 million on the

The statue of the Buddha on the summit of Mount Emei, in the Sichuan Province.

A large and fast-growing metropolis, Wuhan, in eastern China, is home to 10.2 million people.

Yangtze River. The city has grown big so fast that workers are building a new subway system with nearly 140 miles (225 km) of track to accommodate commuters. The subway is part of a $120 billion construction project that includes two airport terminals and an office tower half the size of the Empire State Building.

Still, the more China's cities boom, the more they become crowded. Many people live in cramped apartments on tiny streets. Moreover, urban sprawl, wide road networks, and increased **industrialization** have made China one of the most polluted places on the planet. The World Bank estimates that China has sixteen of the world's twenty most polluted cities, and two out of every ten rivers and lakes are unfit for irrigating crops. The smog is so bad in the big cities, including Beijing, that it is a major cause of death. Pollution has contaminated half of China's groundwater.

Despite these problems, many cities, especially Shanghai and Beijing, rival Paris and New York for their vitality. In the city, people leave their old village ties behind. They no longer have to go to the fields to find food. Instead, they walk to the local markets to buy their food and clothing. They listen to modern music, go out dancing, and eat in restaurants. They surf the Internet on laptops in teahouses and play mahjong on street corners.

Although the importance of the cities has increased in recent years, the villages are still the **cornerstone** of Chinese tradition, where distinct ethnic groups thrive. You can see the importance of the villages in architecture and how people dress. Most of these minority groups have their own languages and customs. For example, in the villages of central Guizhou, a province just north of China's border with Vietnam, artisans still weave cloth without machines. Miao (one of China's many ethnic groups) women sew by hand, sometimes taking two years to embroider colorful wedding clothes. They sew their own clothes instead of traveling hundreds of miles to a city store. Like their ancestors, the women still use **indigo** to dye cloth. Miao men have their own age-old traditions, too. They hunt and play traditional instruments such as reed pipes.

COUNTRY LIFE

Although life in the countryside might seem idyllic, it is a hard existence for many. Nearly 18 million poor people live in rural areas, many without electricity, running water, sewage systems, or paved roads. The government says that roughly 128 million of its rural citizens are destitute, subsisting on $1.00 a day—25 cents under the worldwide poverty line.

A group of Miao women in traditional clothing sing during a performance in the Miao Ethnic Minority Village, in the southwestern province of Guizhou.

The Wind and Rain Bridge, located on the Nanjiang River, is an architectural symbol of the Dong ethnic group, who also live in the Guizhou Province.

In Miao villages, as elsewhere, life is dependent on the soil. In many rural villages, houses are still made of wood and are tightly packed together to maximize the land available for farming. The village square, if there is one, is the center of the community, where festivals, markets, and celebrations take place.

Farmers throughout the country generally grow rice and vegetables on the same small plot of land that their ancestors probably cultivated centuries ago. They produce enough to eat but not much to sell. Most live in simple bamboo, straw, or wood houses with dirt floors. Houses with more than two stories are rare. Seldom are there running water or toilets. People cook outside on open fires. While some villages have refrigerators, televisions, and even washing machines, they can run them only at night because nearby factories need the electricity during the day.

The Dong people, one of the largest ethnic groups in China, still live in the tree-lined hills along the Hunan-Guizhou-Guangxi border. Each village has between twenty and thirty houses built near rivers and streams. These houses are usually made from wood and are often several stories tall. The Dong live in the upper floors, while their domesticated animals, goats, cows, and chickens crowd the lower level. Often towering over Dong villages are massive drum towers that look out on the verdant hills. Some are thirteen stories high and shaped like octagons. The towers serve as meeting places and a venue to hold public ceremonies and celebrations.

Rural villages are also **bastions** of traditional song, music, art, theater, cuisine, and religion. Scholars say such culture could vanish as the villages lose residents to the cities. They point to a village called Lei Family Bridge near Beijing, where a group of musicians once played for the pilgrims who traveled north to Mount Yajia and west to Mount Miaofeng—both holy mountains.

THE PEOPLE OF CHINA

There are fifty-six ethnic groups in China, the largest of which are the Han. Han make up 91 percent of China's population. They live in almost every part of China. They dress in Western-style garb, although a few wear the traditional *hanfu*, which consists of long skirts called *chang* and deep, flowing sleeves.

The performers played traditional music based on stories from nearly 800 years ago. In 2009, the government razed the village to make way for a golf course, which never was built. The village's residents, including the musicians, scattered. Still, they continued to gather under the bridge once a week to serenade the pilgrims, a difficult task because most live miles away. As the performers get older, however, young people are refusing to take their place in the **ensemble**. They are distracted by computers, movies, and televisions—and the allure of city life.

Women in traditional Han dress take part in the Peony Festival in the Heibei Province.

TEXT-DEPENDENT QUESTIONS

1. How is city life in China different from rural life?
2. How will migration from villages to the city impact China's culture?
3. Why are younger people eager to leave the villages for the cities?

RESEARCH PROJECTS

1. Go to the library or use the Internet to research a minority group in China. Write an essay focusing on their history, their culture, and their traditions.
2. Imagine that you are planning a trip to China. Create an itinerary of the places you want to see. Be as detailed as you can and explain why you are eager to travel to these sites.

Terraced rice fields in the Yao Village in China's southern Guangxi Province.

FURTHER RESEARCH

Online

Visit the Central Intelligence Agency's World Factbook about China for statistics about the country, a brief history, and maps: https://www.cia.gov/library/publications/the-world-factbook/geos/ch.html.

Discover more about tourism in China on the China Like Never Before website: http://www.cnto.org.

Learn more about traveling in China, as well as other interesting information, by visiting the China Travel Guide website: http://travelchinaguide.com.

Books

Carter, Tom. *China: Portrait of a People*. Hong Kong: Blacksmith Books, 2010.

Fallows, Deborah. *Dreaming in Chinese: Mandarin Lessons in Life, Love, and Language*. New York: Walker & Company, 2011.

Liu, Junru. *Chinese Food*. 3rd ed. Cambridge, UK: Cambridge University Press, 2011.

Wenzhong, Hu. *Encountering the Chinese: A Modern Country, An Ancient Culture*. 3rd ed. Boston: Intercultural Press, 2010.

Zee, Anthony. *Swallowing Clouds: A Playful Journey through Chinese Culture, Language, and Cuisine*. Seattle: University of Washington Press, 2014.

NOTE TO EDUCATORS: This book contains both imperial and metric measurements as well as references to global practices and trends in an effort to encourage the student to gain a worldly perspective. We, as publishers, feel it's our role to give young adults the tools they need to thrive in a global society.

SERIES GLOSSARY

ancestral: relating to ancestors, or relatives who have lived in the past.

archaeologist: a scientist that investigates past societies by digging in the earth to examine their remains.

artisanal: describing something produced on a small scale, usually handmade by skilled craftspeople.

colony: a settlement in another country or place that is controlled by a "home" country.

commonwealth: an association of sovereign nations unified by common cultural, political, and economic interests and traits.

communism: a social and economic philosophy characterized by a classless society and the absence of private property.

continent: any of the seven large land masses that constitute most of the dry land on the surface of the earth.

cosmopolitan: worldly; showing the influence of many cultures.

culinary: relating to the kitchen, cookery, and style of eating.

cultivated: planted and harvested for food, as opposed to the growth of plants in the wild.

currency: a system of money.

demographics: the study of population trends.

denomination: a religious grouping within a faith that has its own organization.

dynasty: a ruling family that extends across generations, usually in an autocratic form of government, such as a monarchy.

ecosystems: environments where interdependent organisms live.

endemic: native, or not introduced, to a particular region, and not naturally found in other areas.

exile: absence from one's country or home, usually enforced by a government for political or religious reasons.

feudal: a system of economic, political, or social organization in which poor landholders are subservient to wealthy landlords; used mostly in relation to the Middle Ages.

globalization: the processes relating to increasing international exchange that have resulted in faster, easier connections across the world.

gross national product: the measure of all the products and services a country produces in a year.

heritage: tradition and history.

homogenization: the process of blending elements together, sometimes resulting in a less interesting mixture.

iconic: relating to something that has become an emblem or symbol.

idiom: the language particular to a community or class; usually refers to regular, "everyday" speech.

immigrants: people who move to and settle in a new country.

indigenous: originating in and naturally from a particular region or country.

industrialization: the process by which a country changes from a farming society to one that is based on industry and manufacturing.

SERIES GLOSSARY

integration: the process of opening up a place, community, or organization to all types of people.

kinship: web of social relationships that have a common origin derived from ancestors and family.

literacy rate: the percentage of people who can read and write.

matriarchal: of or relating to female leadership within a particular group or system.

migrant: a person who moves from one place to another, usually for reasons of employment or economic improvement.

militarized: warlike or military in character and thought.

missionary: one who goes on a journey to spread a religion.

monopoly: a situation where one company or state controls the market for an industry or product.

natural resources: naturally occurring materials, such as oil, coal, and gold, that can be used by people.

nomadic: describing a way of life in which people move, usually seasonally, from place to place in search of food, water, and pastureland.

nomadic: relating to people who have no fixed residence and move from place to place.

parliament: a body of government responsible for enacting laws.

patriarchal: of or relating to male leadership within a particular group or system.

patrilineal: relating to the relationship based on the father or the descendants through the male line.

polygamy: the practice of having more than one spouse.

provincial: belonging to a province or region outside of the main cities of a country.

racism: prejudice or animosity against people belonging to other races.

ritualize: to mark or perform with specific behaviors or observances.

sector: part or aspect of something, especially of a country's or region's economy.

secular: relating to worldly concerns; not religious.

societal: relating to the order, structure, or functioning of society or community.

socioeconomic: relating to social and economic factors, such as education and income, often used when discussing how classes, or levels of society, are formed.

statecraft: the ideas about and methods of running a government.

traditional: relating to something that is based on old historical ways of doing things.

urban sprawl: the uncontrolled expansion of urban areas away from the center of the city into remote, outlying areas.

urbanization: the increasing movement of people from rural areas to cities, usually in search of economic improvement, and the conditions resulting this migration.

INDEX

Italicized page numbers refer to illustrations.

A

agriculture 9, 14, 36, 53
air and water quality 51
ancestor worship 18, *18*
archaeology *12*, 26
architecture 50–53, *53*
automobile production 37

B

bahe (tug-of-war) 44
banquets 29
Beijing *15*, *21*, 50–51
Beijing Opera 42–43, *43*, 47
birth rate 21, 23
Bodhidharma 46
Boxer Rebellion (1899–1901) 13, 15
Boxers (Righteous and Harmonious Fists) 13
breakfast 27
Buddhism 46, 47, 50, *50*
Buddhist sacred mountains 50, 54
building boom *37*, 50–51, *51*
Butterfly Lovers, The (traditional) 44

C

Chiang Kai-shek 14
children 17–19
chopsticks *30*, 30–31
cities 10, *37*, 38, 49–51, 55
Civil War (1945–1949) 14
clothing production 52
college entrance examination *(gaokao)* 35
communism 14
Communist Party 14, 34, 36
Confucianism 11, 22, 30, 31, 45–46
Confucius 10–11, *11*, 17–18, 27
Confucius Institutes 11
cooking methods 28, 30–31
courtship rituals 20, 23
cuju (sport) 44, *44*
cultural identity 11, 13, 47
Cultural Revolution 14, 20

D

dating and romantic relationships 20, *21*, 23
Dong nationality 53, *53*
dragon boat racing 45, *45*
drum towers 53

E

economic reform *(gaige kaifang)* 36
economy 14, 21, 33, 36–38, *37*
education 11, 14, 33–36, *34*, *36*, 39
educational reform 34
elder care 17–19, *18*, *19*, 23, 28
energy industry 37–38
ethnic and regional cuisine 26, *26*, 31, 42
ethnic groups 21, 51–54, 55
exports 13, 14, 25–26, 36–38, *39*

F

face painting *(lianpu)* 43, 47
family roles and traditions *16*, 17–23, *18*, *19*, *20*
Farewell to my Concubine (traditional) *43*
farming 9, 53, *55*
father's role in family 19–20, *20*
Fenghuang *48*
feudal system 13
filial piety *(xiao)* 17–19, *18*, *19*, 23, 28, *29*
Flower Bridges *53*
food and culinary traditions 25–31, *28*
food exports 25–26
Forbidden City *6*, *15*, 50
foreign influence 13
foreign trade 13, 14, 25–26, 36–38
friendship 18, 22

INDEX

G
General Motors 37
geography 7, 9, 12, 15, 49
globalization 38, 46
grain 26, 29
Great Britain 13
Great Leap Forward 14
Great Wall 11, 49
Guangdong cuisine 26
Guizhou Province 52
gunpowder 9, 13

H
Han dynasty 12, 15, 30, *54*
Hangzhou *37*
Han nationality 54
holiday celebrations and traditions 29, 42, 46
Hong Kong *45*
housing and living conditions 38, 51, 52–53
Huang He (Yellow River) 9–10, *10*
Huguang Theatre (Beijing) *43*
Hunan *48*
Hunan cuisine 26

I
immigration 44
imperial rule 11–12, 13, 15
indigo 48, 52
industrialization 14, 36–39, *37*, 50–51
Ireland 30
isolation policy 13, 15

J
Japanese invasion of Manchuria (1931) 14

K
kung fu *40*, 45–47

L
landscape *8*, 49–50
language and writing system 11, *35*, 52
Lantern Festival 44
Lei Family Bridge village 54
leisure activities 41–42
literacy rate 33
Longshan culture 10

M
mahjong 42, *42*
Manchuria 14
Mao Zedong (Mao Tse-Tung) *14*, 14–15, 20, 34
marriage traditions 20, *21*, 23
martial arts *40*, 45–47, *47*
masks 44
matchmaker 20
mealtime traditions *23*, *24*, 27, *29*, 29–31
Miao Ethnic Minority Village (Xijiang) *52*
Miao nationality *52*, 52–53
Mickey Mouse 41
Middle Kingdom (Zhongguo) 9
middle school 35
Ming dynasty 44, 50
minority groups 21, 51–54, 55
modernization 11, 13–14, 46
monarchy 13
Mongolia 13
moon cakes 29, *29*
Moon Festival (Mid-Autumn Festival) 29, *29*
Mount Emei 50, *50*
Mount Miaofeng 54
Mount Yajia 54
Mozi (Master Mo) 27
music 52, *52*, 54

INDEX

N
National Higher Education Entrance Examination 35
Nationalists 14
natural resources 9, 15
Neolithic farming 9
New Year celebration (Spring Festival) 29, 35, 44–46
noodles 25–26, *26*, 29, *31*

O
one-child policy 21, 23
opera 42–44
opium 13, 15
Opium Wars 13, *13*, 15

P
paper and printing 9, 12
pasta 25–26
Peony Festival (Heibei Province) *54*
personal and business relationships 22, *22*
personal and social relationships 22–23
personal reputation *(lian)* 22–23
planned economy 14
pollution 51, *51*
Polo, Marco 25
population growth and distribution 7, 21, 23, 50–51, 55
poverty 52
Pre-Qin period 27
primary schools 35
Protection of the Rights and Interests of Elderly People 19, 23
public works projects 10–12

Q
Qin Shi Huangdi (Zheng) 11–12, *12*
Qu Yuan 45

R
ramen soup *31*
religion 10, 42, 45–47, 50, *50*
Republic of China 13, 34
rice 26–27, *27*, 29, 53, *55*
rural villages 21, 51–54, 55

S
school curriculum 34
Sea World Parks & Entertainment 41
Shang Di 10
Shang dynasty 10
Shanghai *37*, 41, 50–51
Shaolin Monastery *40*, 45–46
shipping 12
Sichuan cuisine 26, *26*
Sichuan opera 44
silk production 10
Silk Road 12
Simpsons, The 46
Six Flags Entertainment Corporation 41
smog 51
soccer 44, *44*
social class system 10–11, 14
soup 29
spaghetti 25
spices in regional cuisine 26
sports *42*, *44*, 44–47, *46*
Spring Festival (New Year celebration) 29, 35, 44–46
steel industry 37, *37*, 38
Summer Olympics (Beijing, 2008) 35
Sun Yat-Sen 13

T
table tennis 46, *46*
tai chi 46, *47*
Tang dynasty 43
Taoism 45–47
tea 29–30, *30*

INDEX

technical innovation 9, 12–13, 36
terra-cotta warriors *12*
theme parks 41
Three Gorges Dam (Hubei Province) 38, *38*
Tibet 13
tombs *12*
tourism *14*, *52*
Toyota Motor Corporation 37
trade routes 12
traditional arts and entertainment 42–44, *44*, 47, 54, 55
traditional dress 52, 54, *54*
transportation system 10–11, *32*, 50–51
Treaty of Tientsin (1858) *13*
Turkey 30

u
United States investment in China 41, 47
urbanization 50–51, 55

v
vassal states 13
Venice 25

w
Walt Disney Company 41
Warner Brothers Entertainment, Inc. 41
warrior monks 46
wedding traditions 29
Wei river 10
Wind and Rain Bridge (Guizhou Province) *53*
World Trade Organization (WTO) 37
World War II 14
Wudi (Han emperor) 12
Wuhan *32*, 50–51, *51*

y
Yangtze River 38, *38*, 50–51
Yao Village *55*
Yellow River (Huang He) 9–10, *10*

z
Zen Buddhism 46
Zheng (Qin Shi Huangdi) 11–12, *12*
Zhongguo (Middle Kingdom) 9
Zhongshan Iron Bridge *10*
Zhou dynasty 10
Zi Lu 17–18

PHOTO CREDITS

Page	Page Location	Archive/Photographer
6-7	Full page	Dreamstime/Patrck Lau
8	Top	Dollar Photo Club/curioustravelers
10	Bottom left	Dollar Photo Club/suronin
11	Top right	Dollar Photo Club/babara_r
12	Top	Dollar Photo Club/V. ZHURAVLEV
13	Top right	Wikimedia Commons/Laurence Oliphant
14	Bottom	Wikimedia Commons/Brücke-Osteuropa
15	Bottom	Dollar Photo Club/V. ZHURAVLEV
16	Top	Dollar Photo Club/szeyuen
18	Top	Dollar Photo Club/lapas77
19	Bottom	iStock.com/OSTILL
20	Top	iStock.com/duncan1890
21	Bottom	Dollar Photo Club/xixinxing
22	Top left	iStock.com/XiXinXing
23	Bottom	iStock.com/XiXinXing
24	Top	Dollar Photo Club/Monkey Business
26	Bottom	Dollar Photo Club/sasaken
27	Top right	Dollar Photo Club/uckyo
28	Bottom	Dreamstime/Julie Feinstein
29	Top right	Dreamstime/Shannon Fagan
29	Bottom left	Dollar Photo Club/Andrew Blue
30	Top left	Dollar Photo Club/Jack.Q
30	Bottom right	Dreamstime/Paolo Pagani
31	Bottom	Dollar Photo Club/shima-risu
33	Top	Dreamstime/Huating
34	Top	Dreamstime/Jianbinglee
35	Bottom	Dreamstime/Pixbox
36	Top	Dreamstime/Otnaydur
37	Top right	Dreamstime/Zhaojiankang
37	Bottom	Dreamstime/Cao Hai
38	Top	Dreamstime/Prillfoto
39	Bottom	Dreamstime/Christineg
40	Top	Dreamstime/Linqong
42	Top left	Dreamstime/Lee Snider
42	Top right	Dreamstime/Lee Snider
43	Bottom	Dreamstime/Hungchungchih
44	Bottom left	Baidu
45	Top	Dreamstime/Mike K.
46	Bottom left	Dreamstime/Li Lin
47	Bottom	Dreamstime/Hse0193
49	Top	Dreamstime/Lizu Zhao
50	Bottom left	Dreamstime/Pytyczech
51	Top	Dreamstime/Gjp311
52	Bottom	Dreamstime/Ying Liu
53	Top	Dreamstime/Hse0193
54	Bottom	Dreamstime/Jianbinglee
55	Bottom	Dreamstime/Vladimir Grigorev

COVER

Top	Dreamstime/Sofiaworld
Bottom left	Dollar Photo Club/Lonely Crane
Bottom right	Dreamstime/Dashark

ABOUT THE AUTHOR

John Perritano is an award-winning journalist, writer, and editor from Southbury, Connecticut, who has written numerous articles and books on history, culture, and science for publishers that include National Geographic's *Reading Expedition Series* and its *Global Issues Series*, focusing on such topics as globalization, population, and natural resources. He has also been a contributor to Discovery.com, *Popular Mechanics*, and other magazines and websites. He holds a master's degree in American History from Western Connecticut State University.